Coloring book for girls

We offer you a premium version full of girls' artistic creativity.
We were creative in drawing and now you have to show your creativity and skill in coloring.

BE CREATIVE. BE CONFIDENT. BELIEVE IN YOURSELF

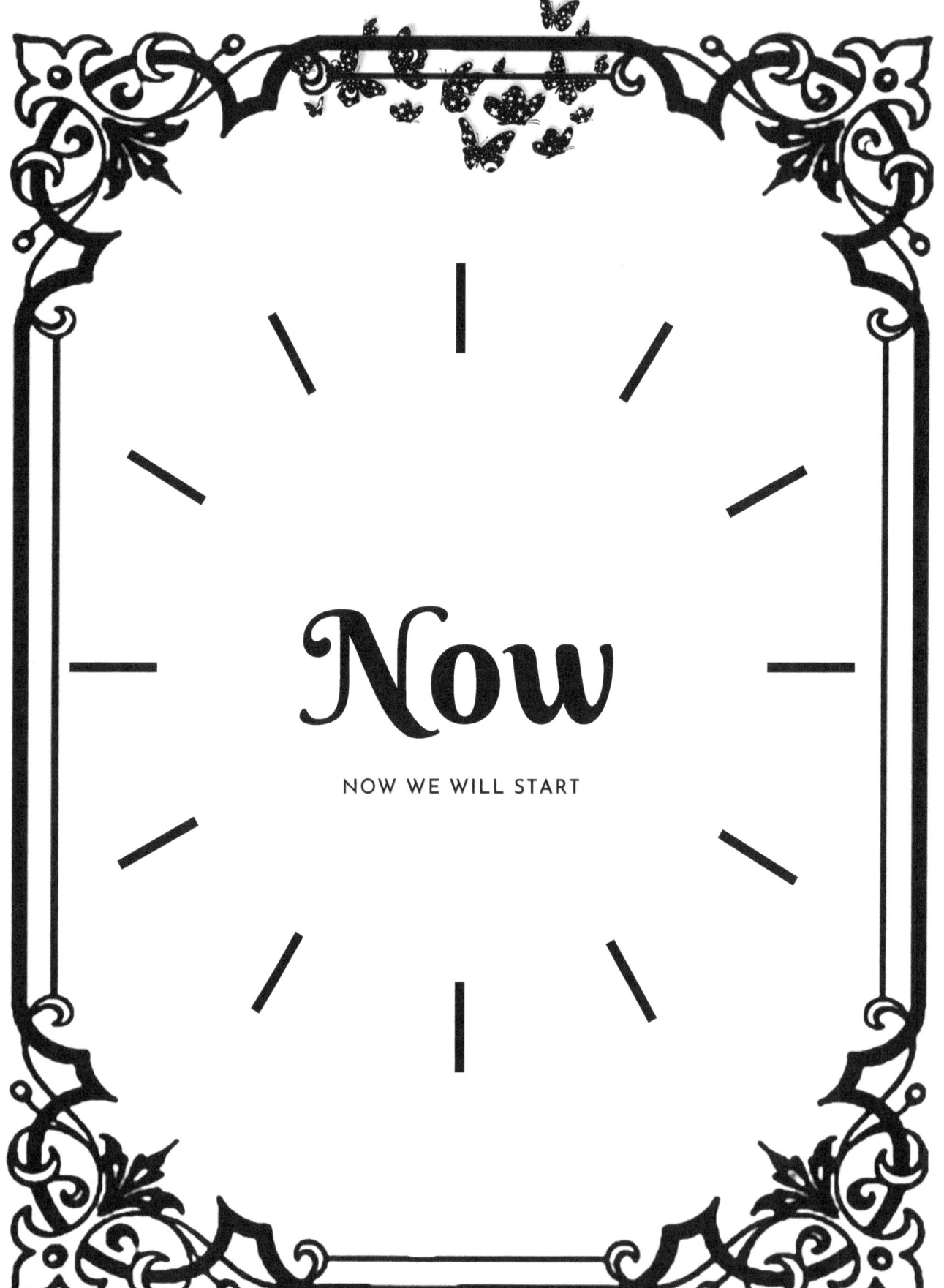

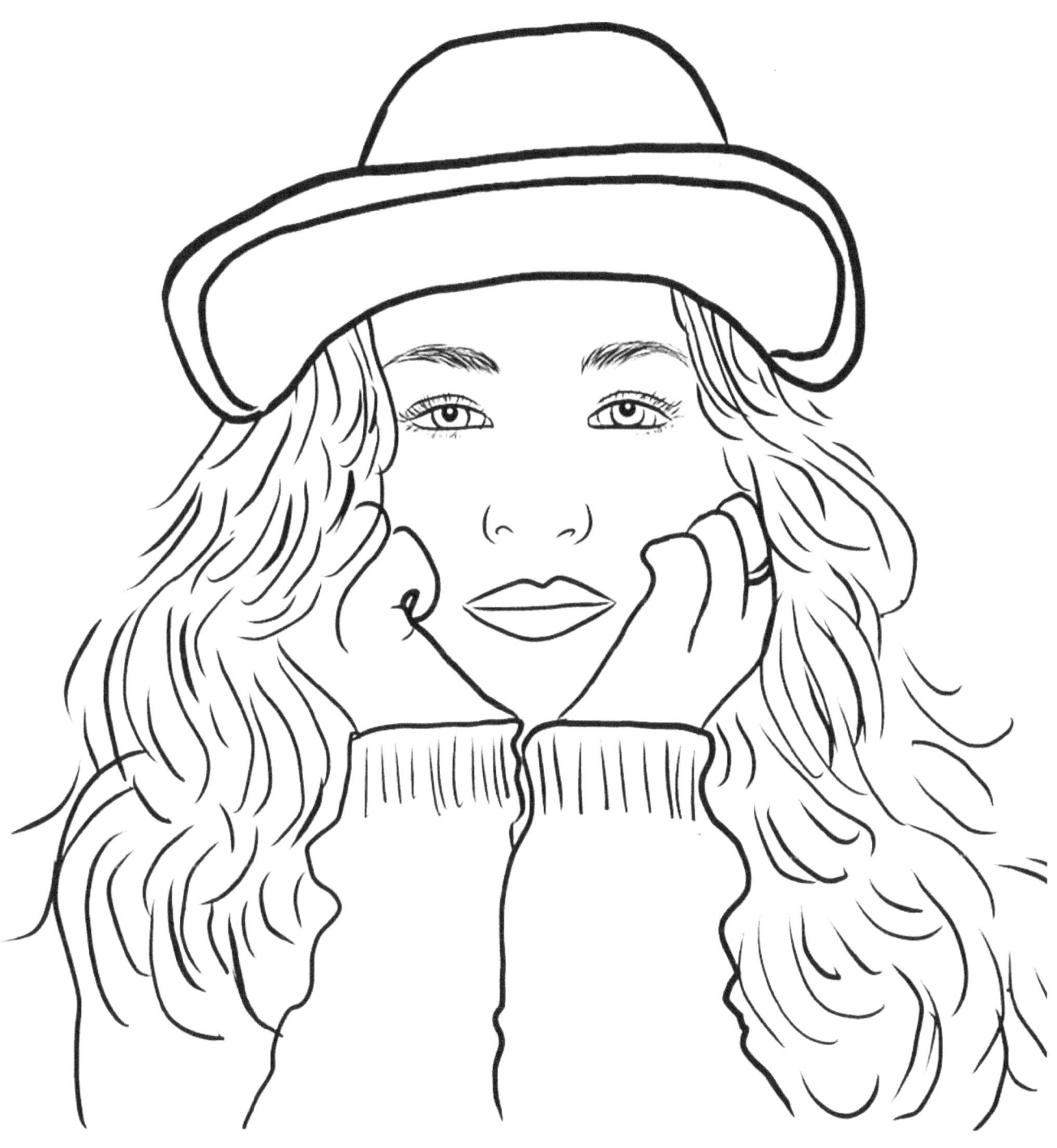

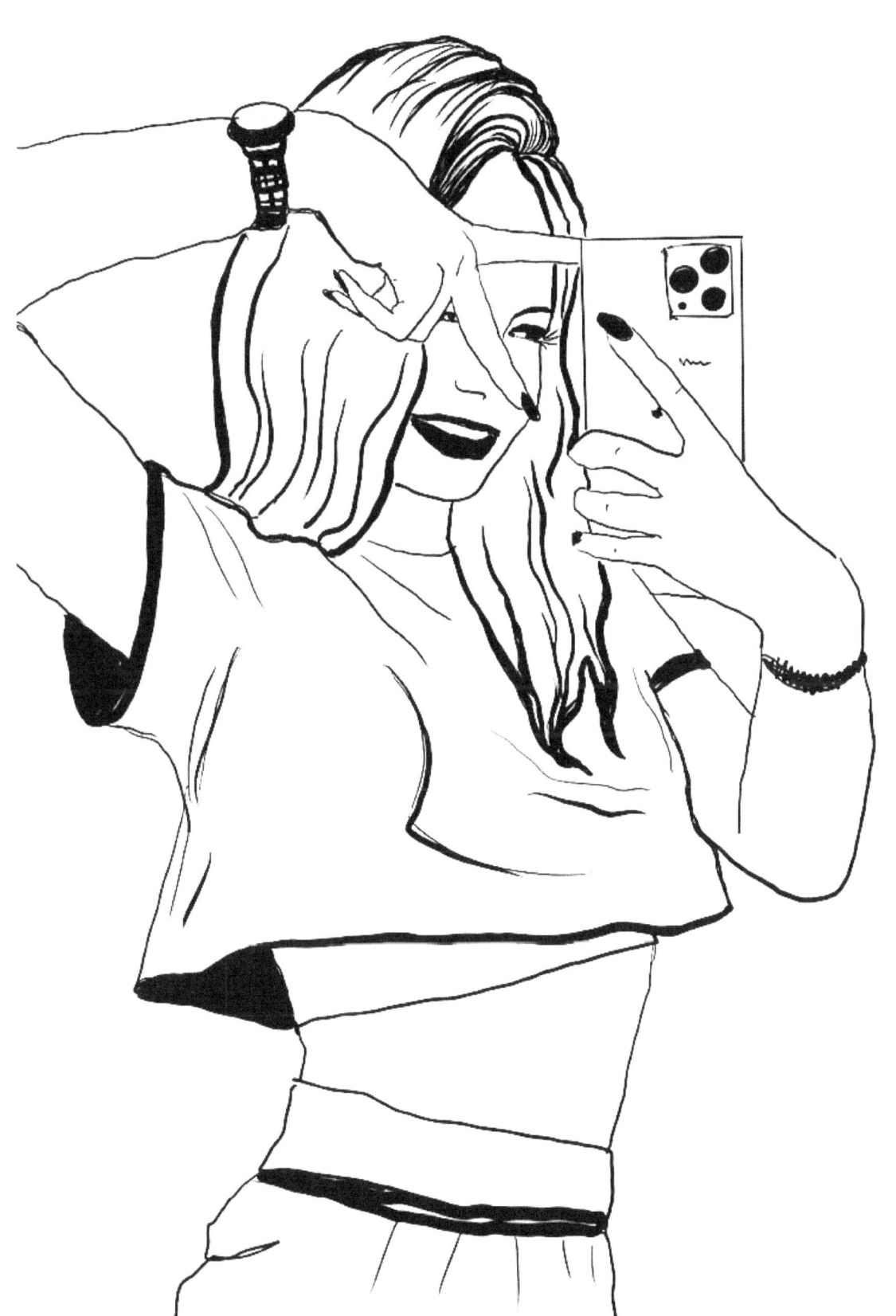

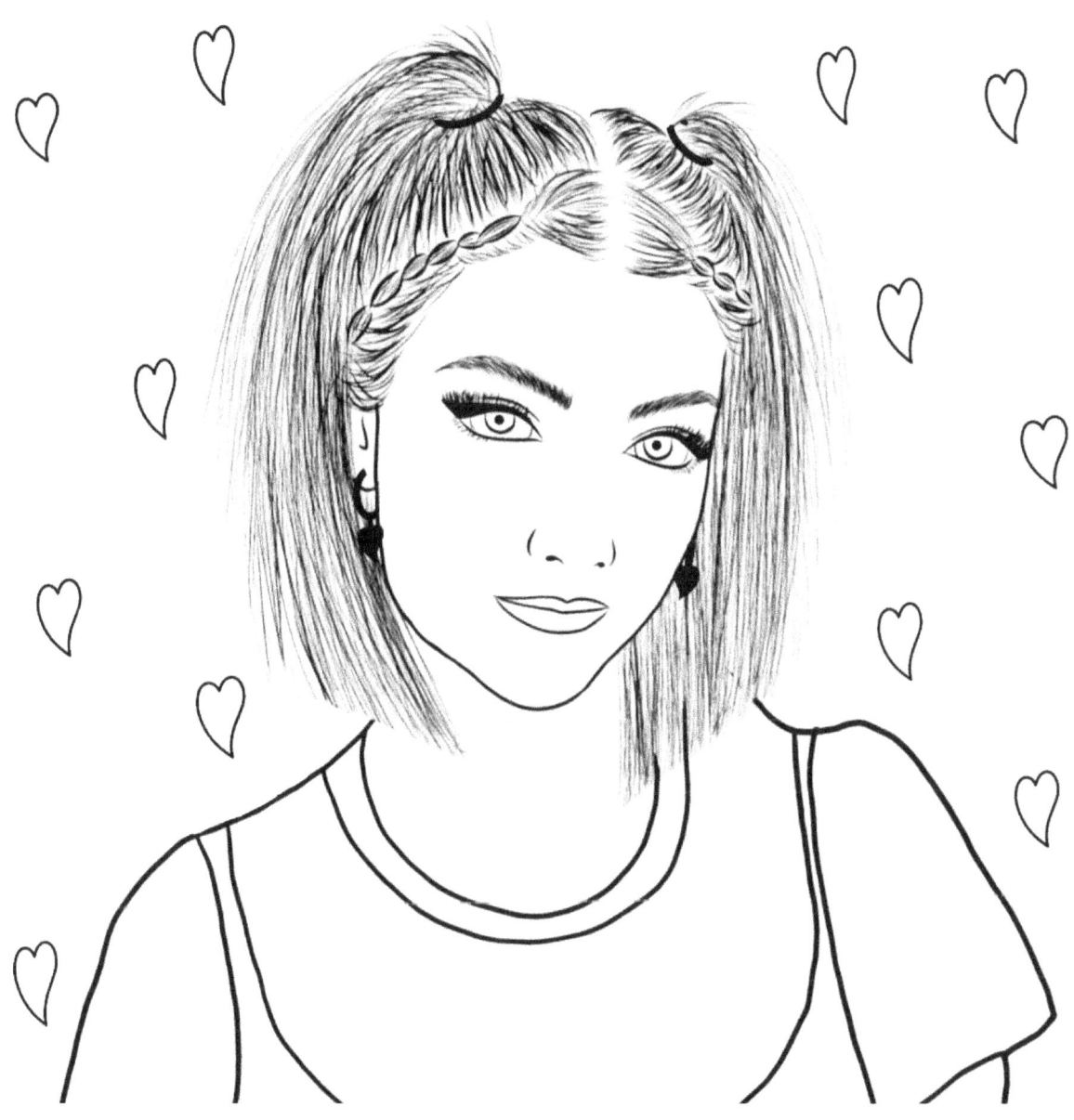

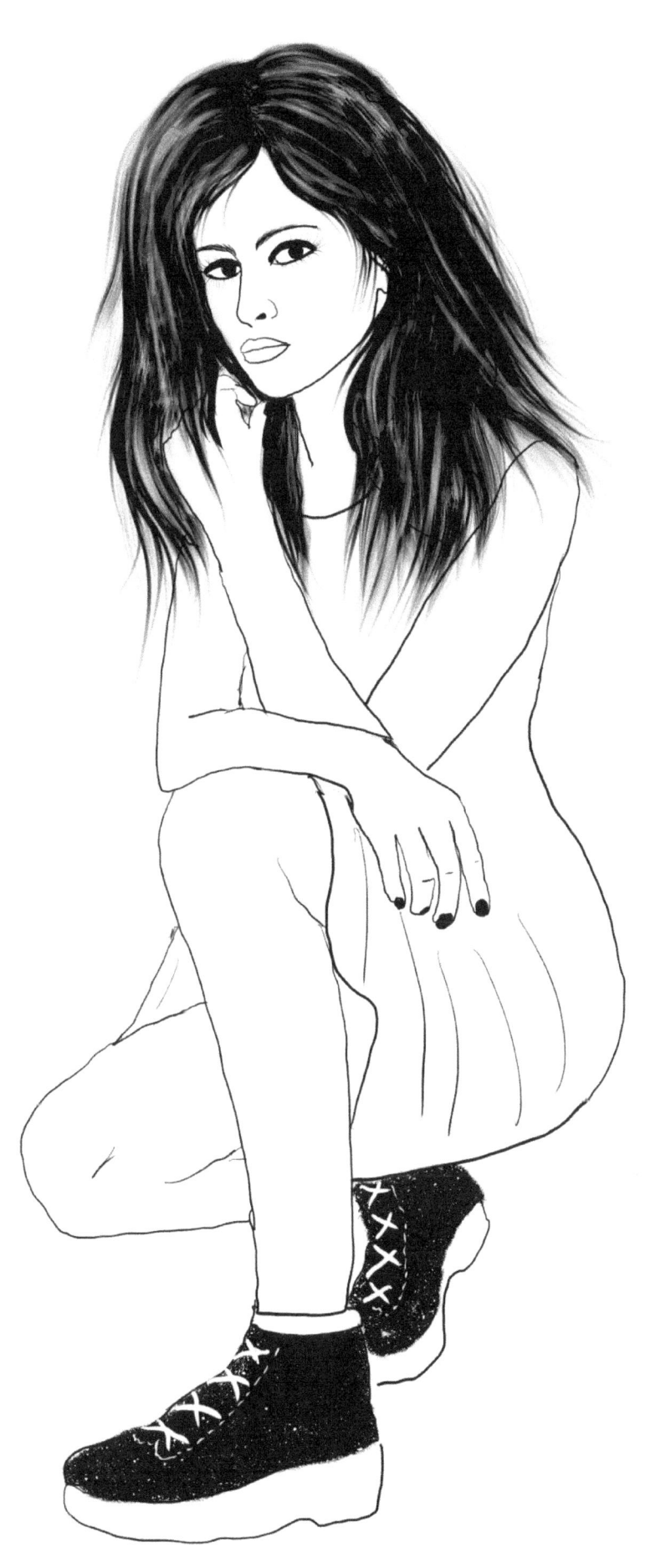

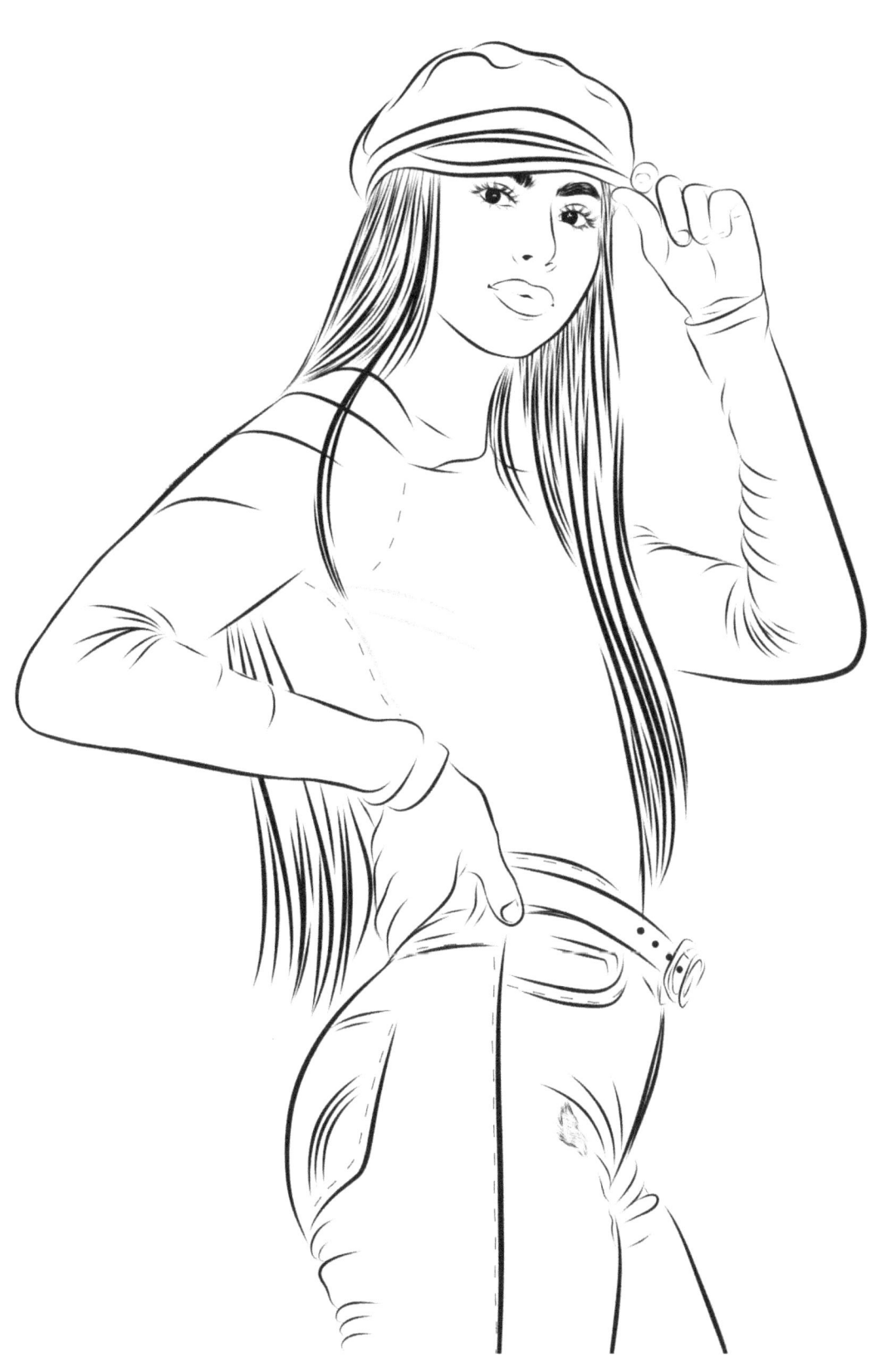

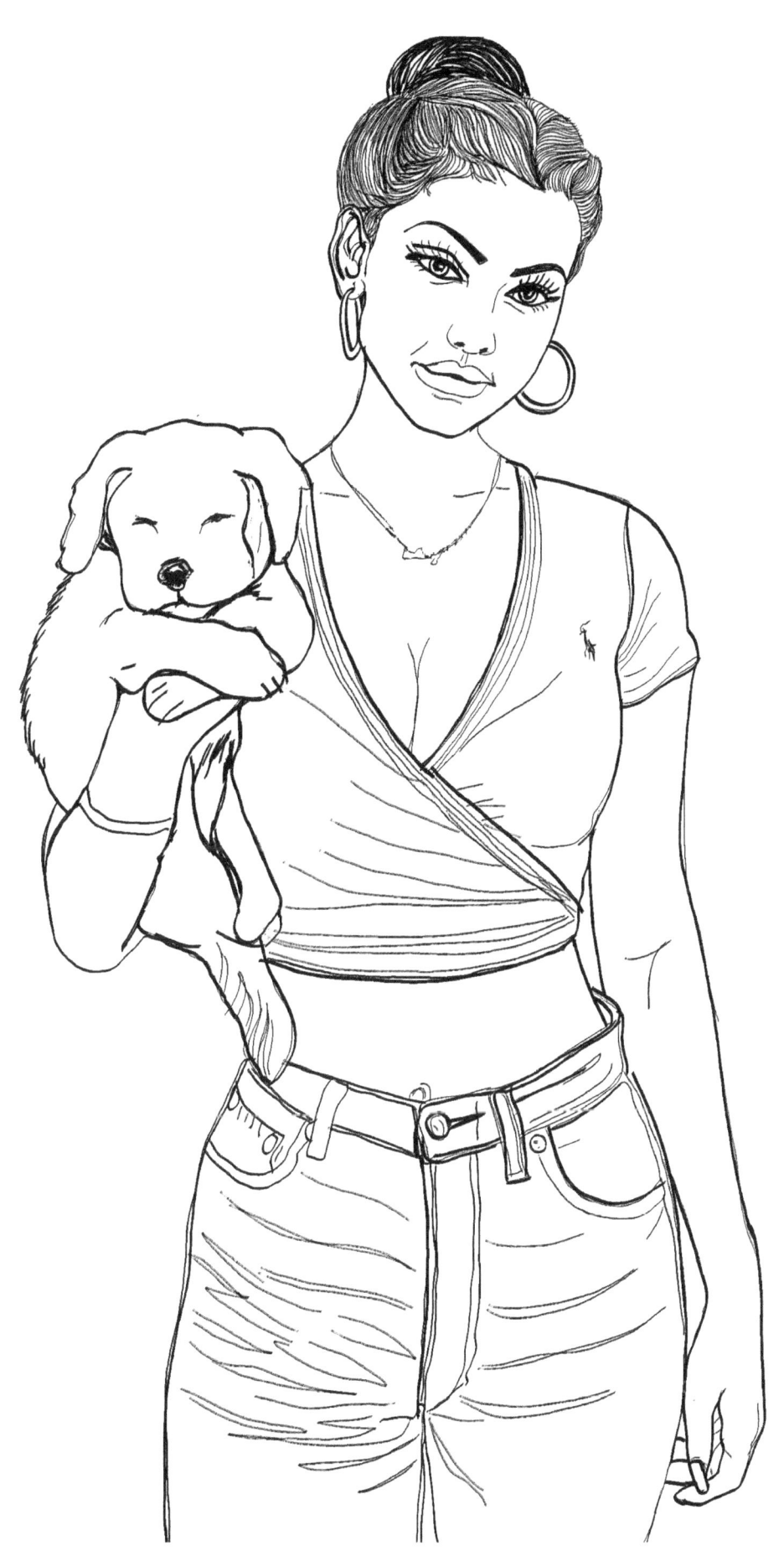

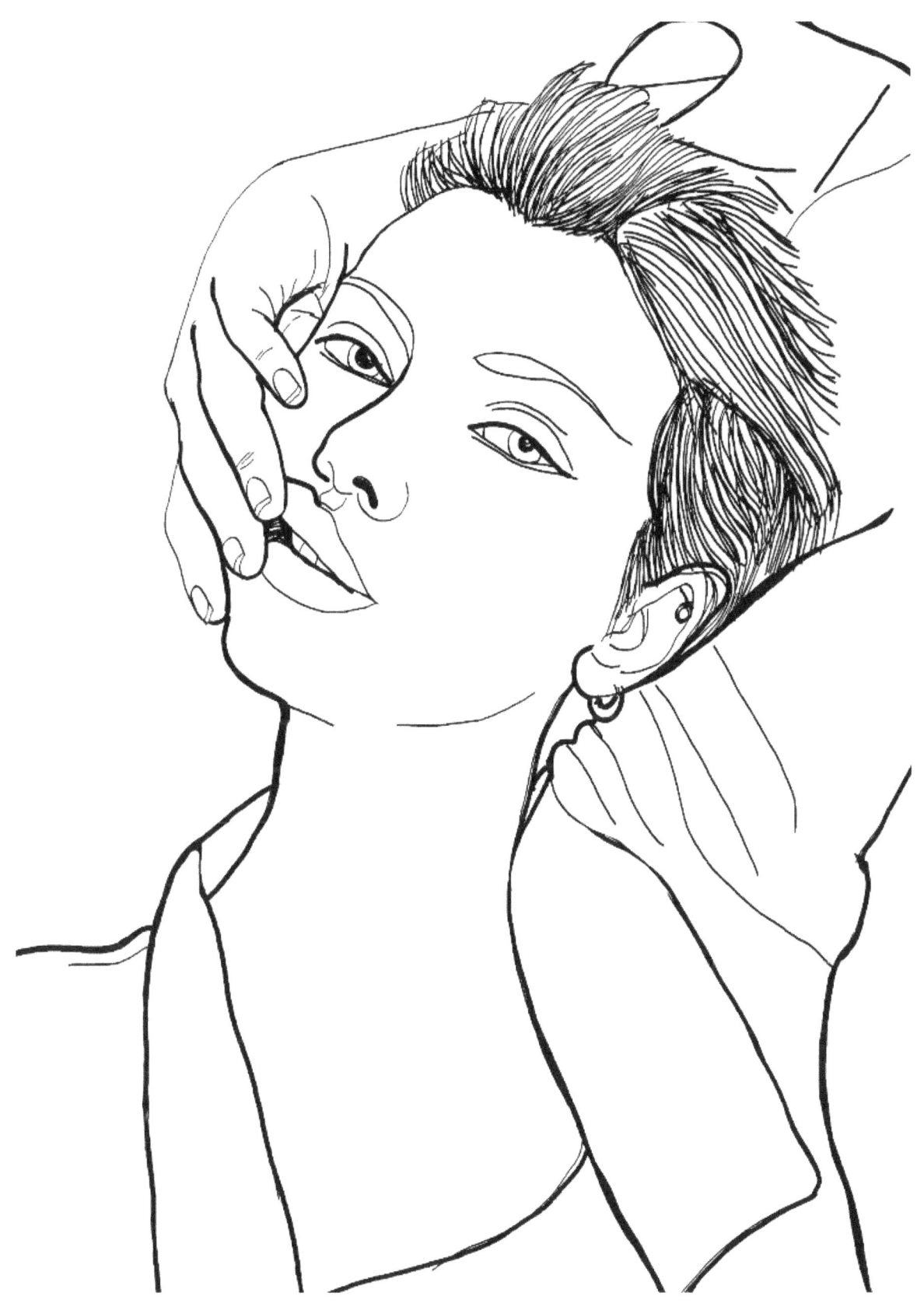

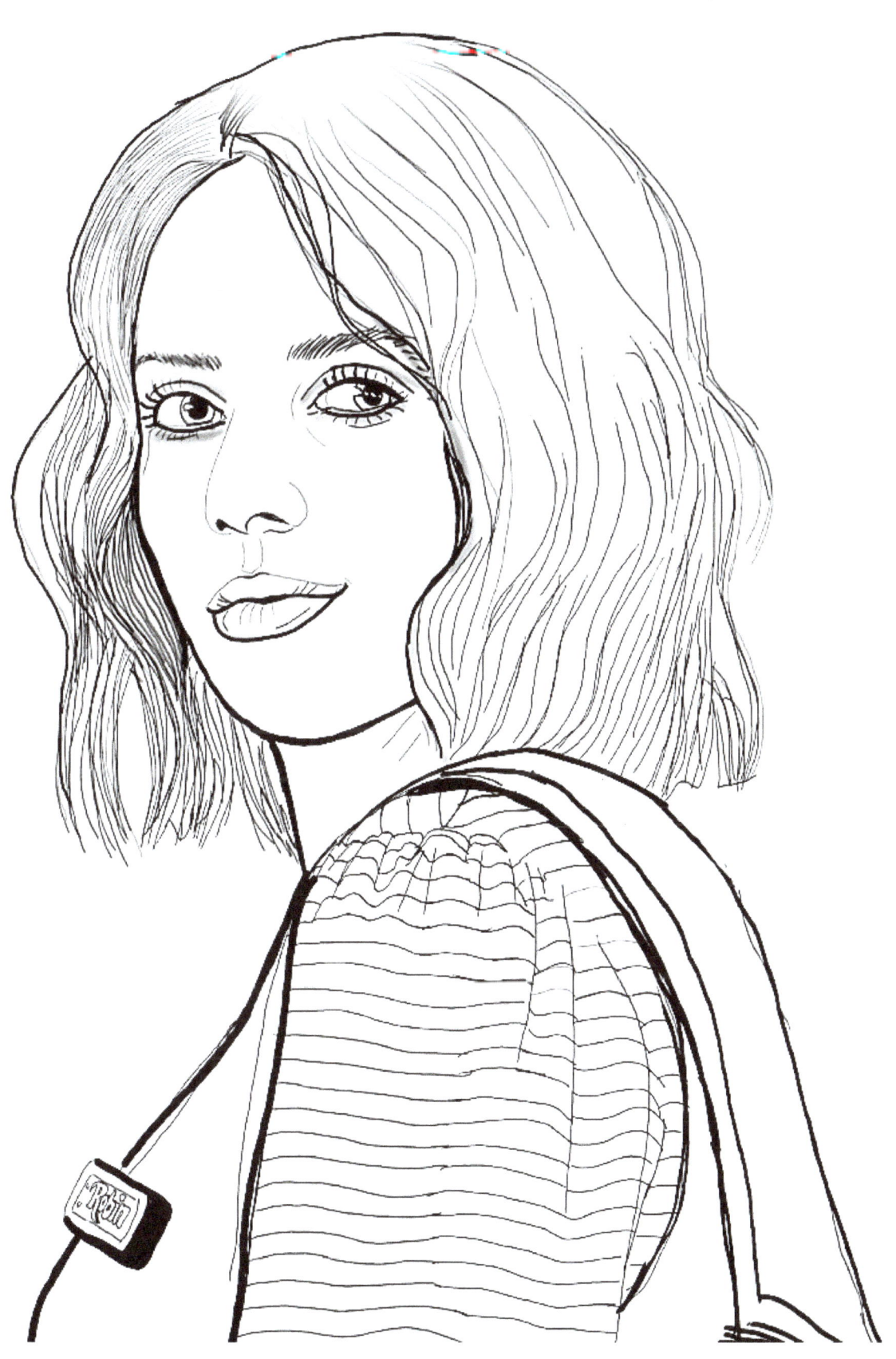

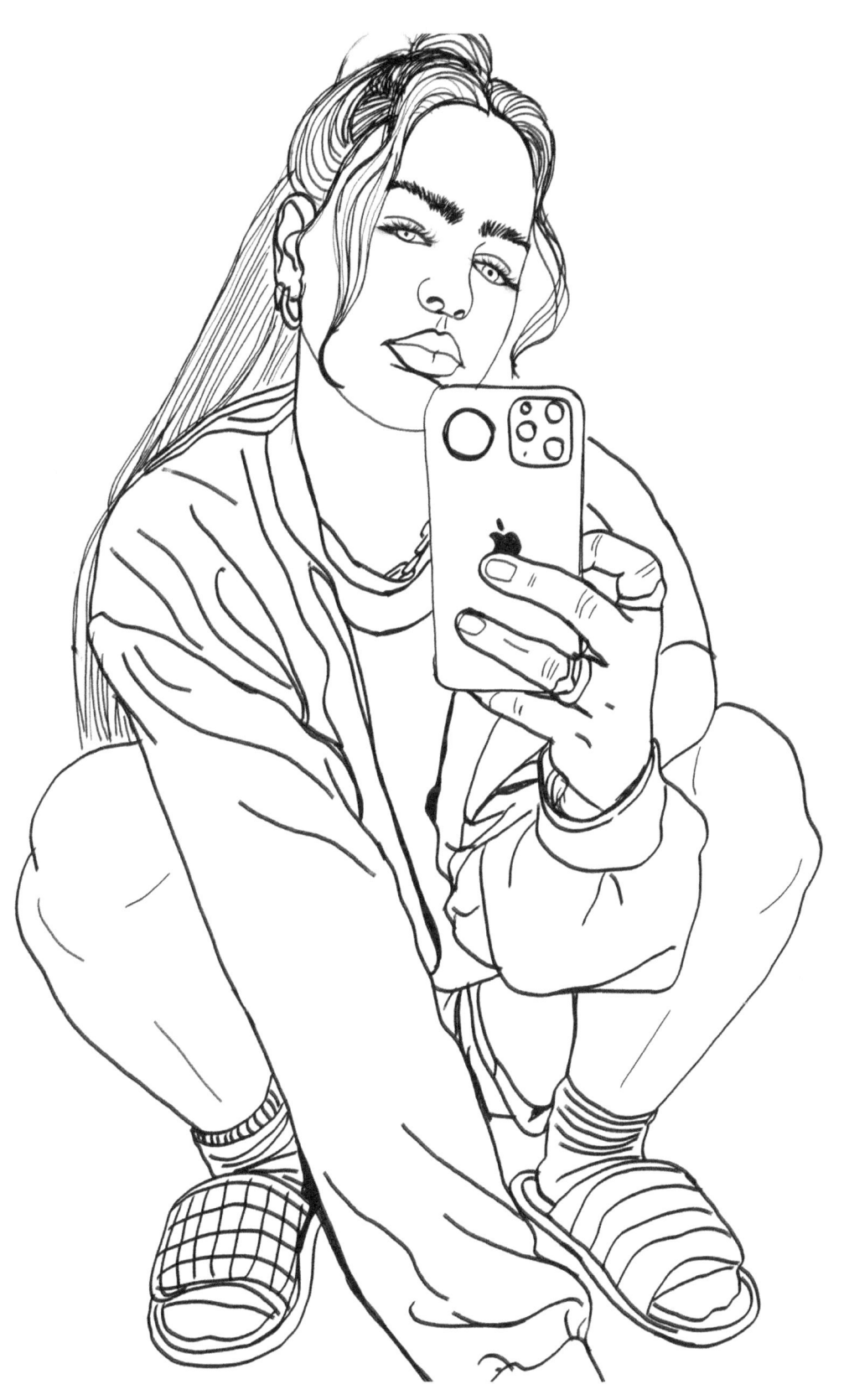

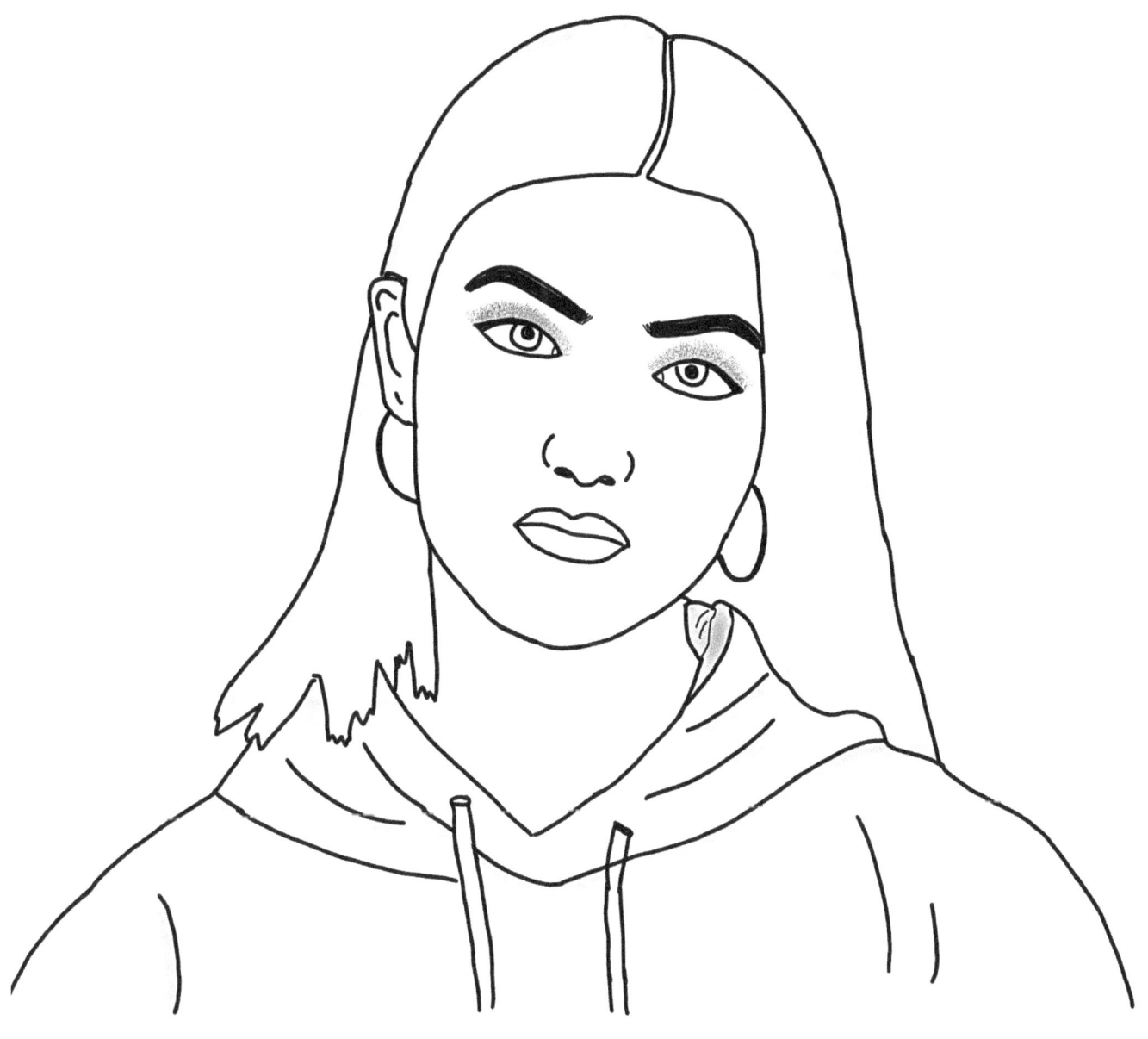

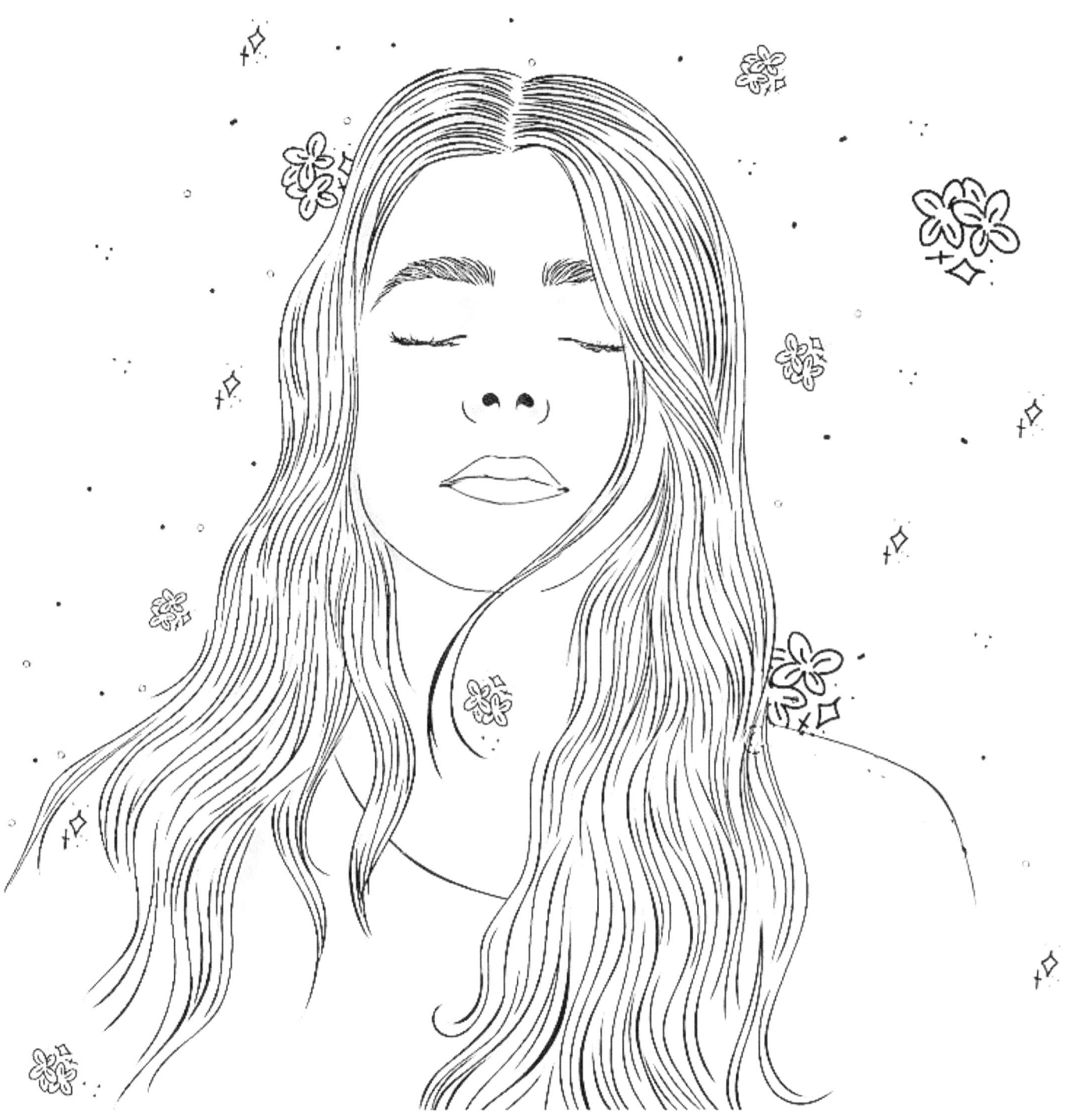

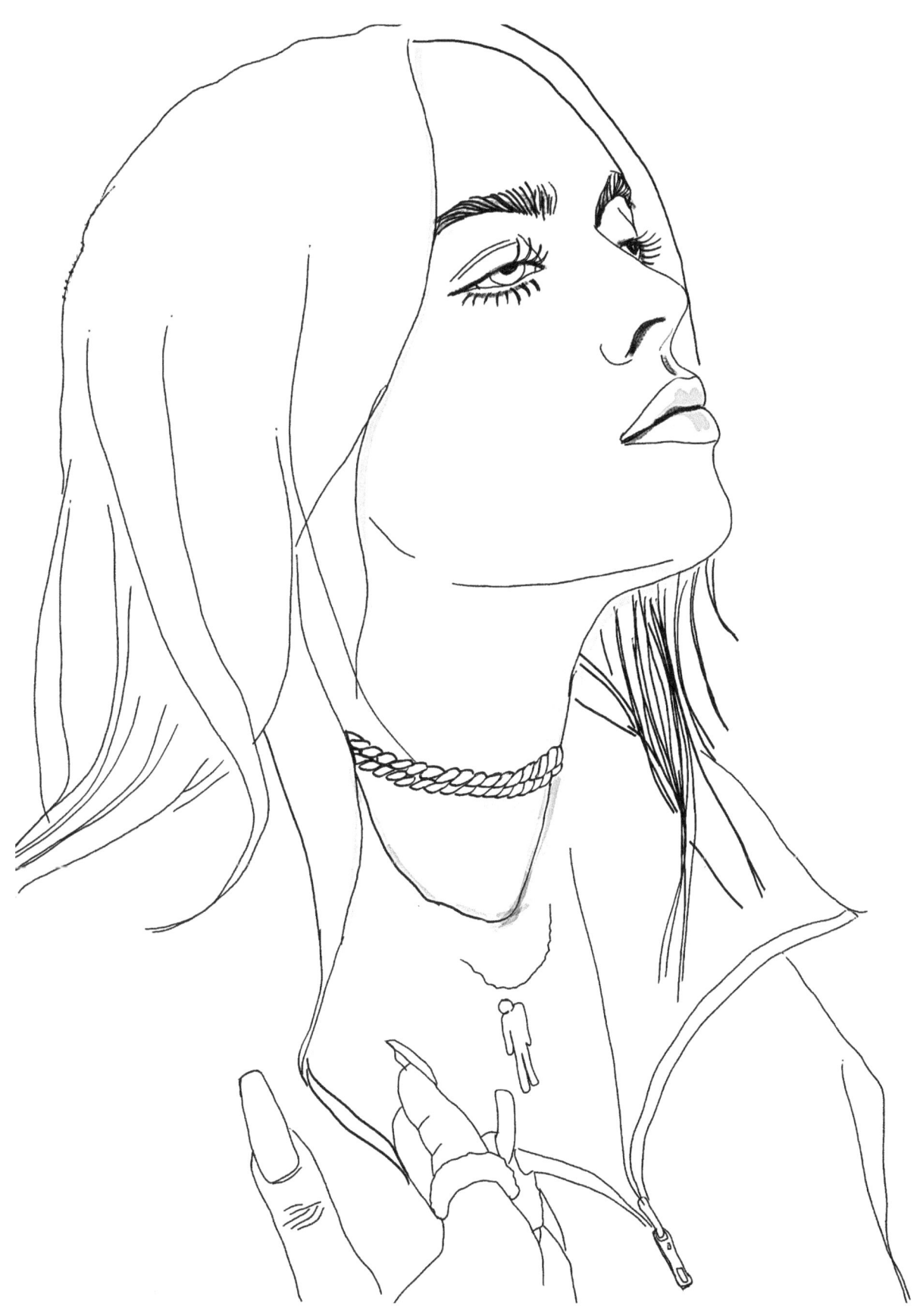

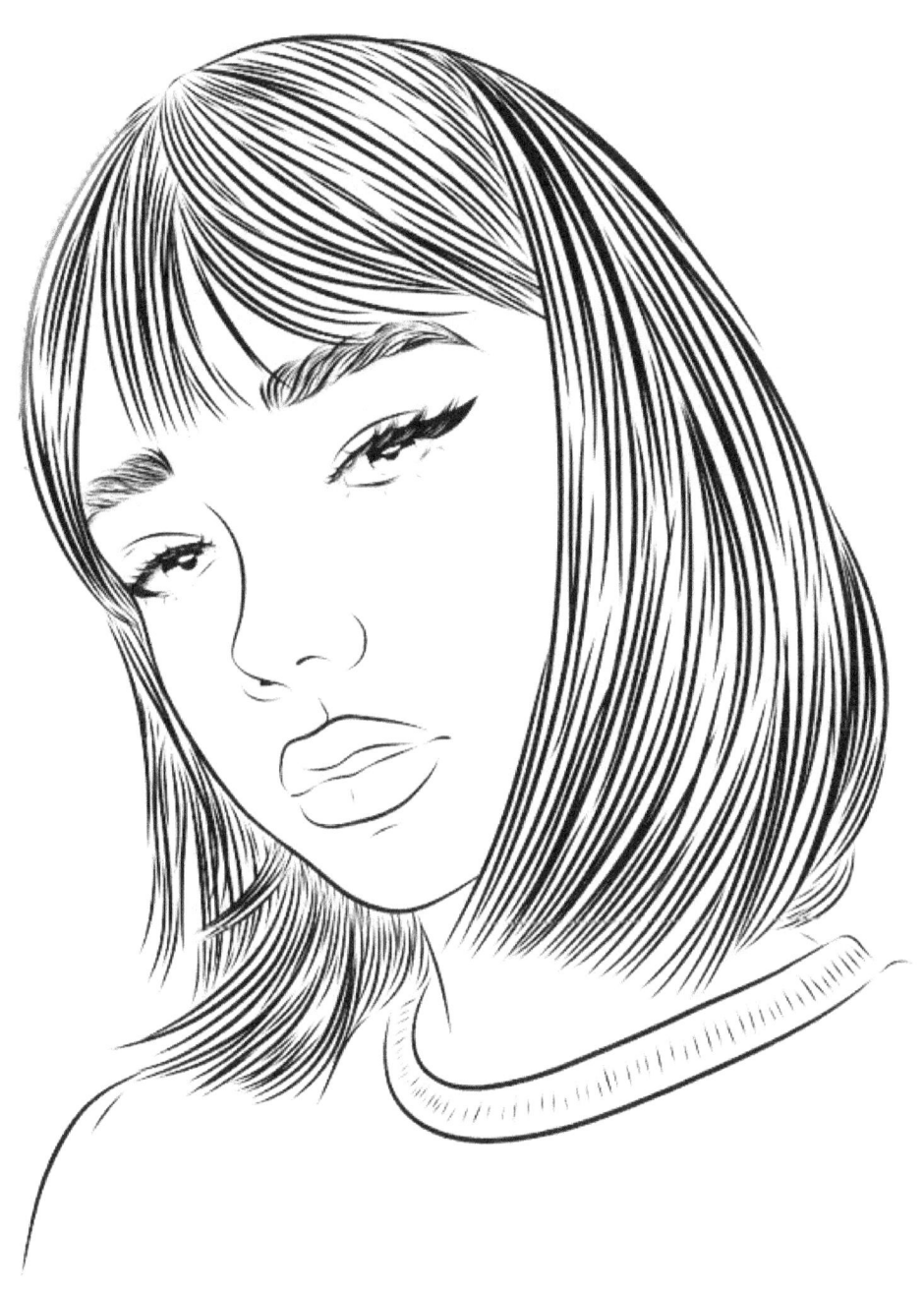

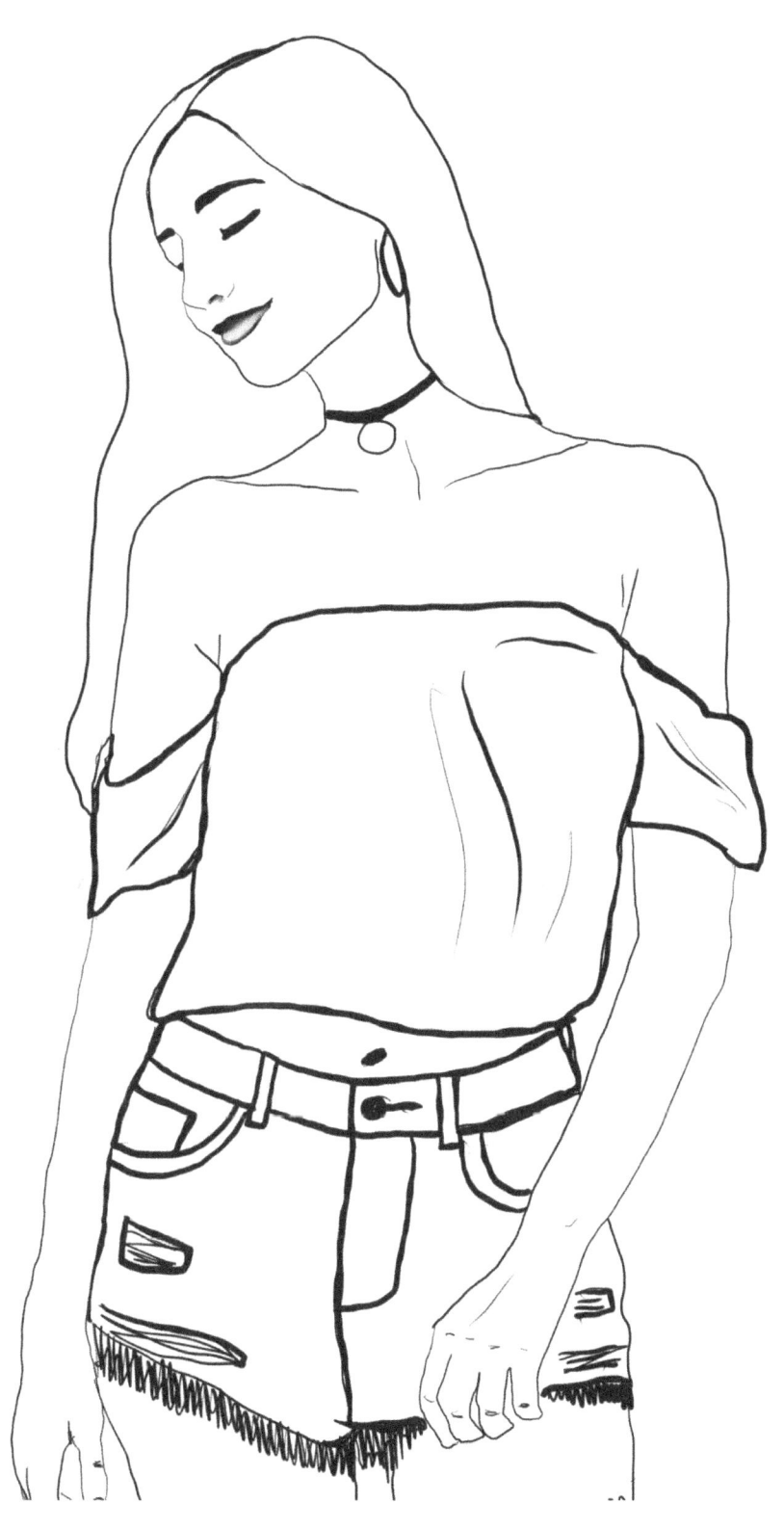

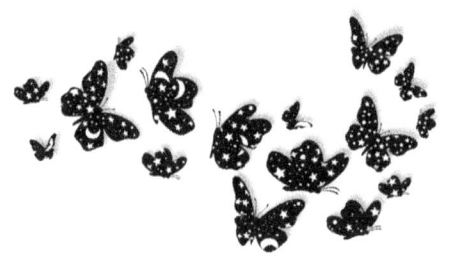

BE
BRAVE

www.ingramcontent.com/pod-product-compliance
Lightning Source LLC
Chambersburg PA
CBHW080439220526
45465CB00009B/3350